Lest I Know Your Weakness

an erasure poetry collection

by

Taylor Ramage

Preface

Erasure poetry is a form of found poetry in which you take a source text, such as a book or newspaper article, and select a few words, phrases, or letters from the page. Then, you "erase" the rest and you're left with a poem. For this collection, I used Joseph Sheridan Le Fanu's 1872 novella *Carmilla*, which is in the public domain. The story is about a young girl named Laura who lives peacefully on a private, isolated estate with her father until a carriage crash on the road brings a mysterious stranger, Carmilla Karnstein, into her life. Carmilla is a vampire, and she and Laura develop a relationship that is sometimes sweet and other times disturbing.

I looked at each page of this story, transposed the found words and letters I saw into a blank document, and organized the poems into a collection structured as a loose dialogue between Laura and Carmilla.

I

Laura

I remember
kissing the strange woman and
assuring her that
for Jesus' sake I often
repeat myself
in a lofty fashion
I forget all my life preceding that event

I was charmed with her
graceful hands
and her sweet low voice
Heavens! If I had but known
her mother, her history
everything in fact connected with her life
but I really could not help it
Her name was Carmilla
Her family was very ancient and noble
Her home lay in my caresses
and her promises
could not offend my ear

II

Carmilla

such rhapsody
she would press me more closely
and kiss gently my agitations
like a lullaby in my ear
she entranced me with
her mysterious excitement
ever and anon I
thought of love growing into adoration
and also abhorrence

This paradox I now write
with a trembling hand
I pass my story to her
and after an hour of apathy
am renewed again and again
breathing so fast that
roses
travel along my cheeks
she whispers

you and I are small but
extraordinary

I break out of suppressed instinct and emotion
a storybook could boast of no such
gallantry as this
her eyes follow me
her ways girlish
and her saunter
alludes to
an afternoon under the trees

III

Laura

The mood tonight
is hanging over us
with the sound of
thunder
We advance in curiosity
and clasp hands
every now and then
her eyes lift
with a tender pulse
I hear her say
"Here am I, on a journey of
life and death
for who can say how long.
I dare not delay
my darling
stay with me and my
devotion."

IV

Carmilla

I talk cheerfully
but am not comforted
for I *awfully* frighten
the half-dreaming housekeeper

in the course of that day,
i desired my words to
remember the thoughtful,
sweet face of that
clumsy girl
after all
the scenes I described
isolated darkness

so i may ramble
but I hope
this charming girl
can promise me
one curious evening

V

Laura

There is no particular reason why I should not tell
you
I hope I have not done a very foolish thing
You, the princess in black velvet
came to me and desired nothing more than
my slender pretty figure
enveloped in soft silk
I remained with you and your dimpling cheeks
what a happiness it was to me

VI

Carmilla

You do not know how dear you are to me
But I dare not tell you
How your wild whims and fancies
charm me
I see it all through a rippling,
transparent night
Love will have sacrifices
I feel so lazy and your pretty prayers
casually come out in careless dreams
light up the dark
please,
laugh at that strange agony

VII

Laura

our violent entrance struck
the utterly puzzled housekeeper
It was past four o'clock, and I
discovered myself in Carmilla's ecstasy
I kissed and embraced her again and again
"Last night has been a night of wonders," she said.
I know I am easily overwhelmed
but Carmilla forgives me

VIII

Carmilla

one time
I thought about
a castle for us
with coffee and chocolate and
candles
you are I think
the prettiest creature I ever saw
look from the window to me
with gleaming eyes and teeth set
as if in fury
may I dare say
we are scarcely alone

IX

Laura

my quaint little Karnstein
overlooks the silent ruins
she is striking and melancholy and I
am only nineteen
but I remember the dinner party
and becoming lost among her
fairy tales
the flicker of an expiring candle
insulted my wonder
She caressed me at the same moment
and whispered
Lay your hand along that
warm puncture
until every second
is daylight

X

Carmilla

dear
I am no nun
and you will think me very selfish
but love me to death
through my nonsense
for your sake I'll talk like a sage
your colors
would take my life
in rich sensations
after our nights in the world
let us burn through stone walls,
light up dark rooms
or darken light ones
as we sleep

XI

Laura

I beheld Carmilla dressed in black
as she traced imaginary lines
in a dirty little book
opposite to the spot where I
ascertained the existence of
heaven
I have described warmly how I
thank her
at last I know that she
kissed me
as if discovering a secret
to keep from the night

Then, with many smiles
and salutations,
Carmilla seemed to forget the spirits
that infect the imagination
But I am so afraid
of all things in heaven,
in the earth,
and under the earth

lying in bed,
I fancied I saw
a monstrous heart
growing faster and darker
her eyes approached my face
and I felt a pain as if
she had forgotten my vain attempts
to deepen our vivacious spirits

together we felt under my pillow
for my charm
and the moment my fingers touched it
I felt quite certain that
she shall pin delightful dreams to my nightdress
like an antidote against wandering
Carmilla proudly interrupted death
and took gentle possession of my soul
She always suffered more
with every turning point

XII

Carmilla

I took her hand as I spoke
still looking
in some dark cupboard for
her lips
I think we both slipped into our
intimacy
as if we were destined to be drawn
but repulsed
Good night, darling
follow me with a fond and melancholy gaze
i am determined to laugh together
over our momentary horrors

XIII

Laura

At the sight of Carmilla in her first panic
I examined our room
the door still locked
She had discovered one of those secrets
which astounded her in silence
so I embraced her till she said

congratulations and welcome to
my bottle of limitations

sometimes
pain spreads on either side of the road
as you approach a half century

Carmilla opened up among the spacious chambers
with increasing amazement
and clenched hands

XIV

Carmilla

Perfect, my dear
I need not approach the topic now
the marvel in your breath
carried it away

there are so many closets
heavy with mysteries
and your graceful languor
restores my mornings

XV

Laura

I charmed her with
grace and magnificent laughs
I loved her to heaven
but would not quarrel upon any
ancient direction
I worried incessantly
and murmured

if your dear heart bleeds
then I draw near to you
and learn the rapture of
that trusting spirit
visit me in my sleep
as a cold current connected in
a sense of exhaustion
I passed through
a long period of danger
with you and
my eyes were dilated and darkened underneath
but I persisted
My nerves
were seldom sensations invoked in courage

XVI

Carmilla

Long ago
I suffered from weakness
and I dare say
let us talk no more of it or
You would not look in my eyes
and pass round my waist lovingly
with a sigh and a little shudder

Are you afraid, dearest?
afraid to die as
a caterpillar in the world
closeted for some time

we emerge together
as dragons
Nevertheless, life and death are
mysterious states

XVII

Laura

I turned
vexed at the interruption
Carmilla, how can you tell me
you are happier when you
trouble my head about
dying
Tell me nothing about ghosts
sit close
hold my hand
I tremble all over
Hold me, hold me still.

she became like a summer cloud
a momentary wanderer who
dressed in black and carried a
magic lantern
we were stitched together with great
masks attached to our
grotesque compliments

XVIII
Carmilla

I cannot cruelly disappoint you
yet our distant journey
is nowhere distinguished
and with conviction I
beckon you to learn
what speaking with earnestness means
kneel for a moment
as i kiss away the mist

Nothing remains
of sweet assurances

I proceed with a dash of horror
I am a fool for having brought you here
But you burn with curiosity
Not a word
ok
see this agitated hand
somewhere about your neck
it covers you only an inch or two below the edge
You see it now with your own eyes
the beginning

XIX

Laura

what beautiful moonlight
so like the night you came to me
slowly we walk to the drawbridge
thinking of the night you
kissed me silently
you pressed in mine a hand
that trembled
Yes, do give me a little wine
dear Carmilla
lest I know your weakness

all your faith in my
sweet summer evening
is imagined
furnish my daydreams till autumn
for I am very glad, dear, that you never
knew me in the room

XX

Carmilla

our reluctant illusion
is so unnecessary
you wish to know why I tell you
of my silent hometown
but I could drive away
all shock
if we both wish
to know how
we represent Cleopatra with the asps to her bosom
we fade upon the walls
and varied decorations envelope us

What was it that struck me dumb?
the very face which (so fixed in my memory)
suspected what I was thinking
when I first beheld its light
I could not repeat
my staged arrival

XXI

Laura

This journey created our ripping looks
nearly all portraits undergo renovations and
we were smoke and dust
the strange look Carmilla made
dried my worn surface at certain points

I remember it without pride
see
Carmilla is an absolute miracle
living, smiling, ready to speak
I am also something of an artist
and her light and color
ask me to lean back
in contemplation
so I descend in the ruins
miles away
Tomorrow
I will be warmly delivered from this century
It is time to return home
we are unspeakably fatigued
But Carmilla is determined to keep me
extraordinary

XXII

Carmilla

People say I am languid
But after all I am perfectly
myself
I talk a great deal of what I call
infatuations
But my thoughts seem to startle
our little card party
i sit on the sofa
anxiously
for I have been thinking of leaving you
I have given you an infinity of trouble
and
I know you dream of
an evening unaided by advice
But I shall do my best to leave
a thousand kisses with you

XXIII

Laura

Nothing I trust recovers immediately
strangulation begins
I recollect the thrill
which you added to me like a passing afternoon
so this evening
repeat to me in front of the castle
our time eating unripe fruit
in foolish days

I knew you would feel for me
be near me in my years on earth
I assure you this is
an effort
to say
but I am
a magnificent masquerade
with colored lamps and ravishing music
you wander through the silence of
my self
and return our masks
under the castle windows

XXIV
Carmilla

my trepidation
is a thrill which you describe
like the current of a cold stream running against
you
I think my direction
is indispensable
Laura, I know you will ask me
to do better
and come down with you
yet I am lost
I might either lose my life
or do fifty foolish things
to delay tomorrow

XXV

Laura

She met me with evasion
as she opened her lips

elegant and distinguished
I saw death
in the plain evening dress

permit me to say a few words which may interest
her

let us be earnestly lost
in time and
you shall know me
I declare myself
your beautiful thunderbolt
and travel nearly a hundred miles
My perplexities multiply by compulsory strength
which i recover when we meet
without any concealment

XXVI
Carmilla

our angrier passions
resumed our bitterness
we had fallen victim to
indulgence
and justified it with
illusions
I remember when I was like you
but I have learned better
I am not some marvelous
preternatural hero
with a special object in a ruined chapel
you think of me as
a pious sacrilege
which will relieve our earth of monsters
I have to tell you, my dear
Karnstein is a name of great pressures
do not seek to conceal them

XXVII

Laura

if it had not been for that charm
I would have
dropped
my faith in her
"Well, I told you so," said Carmilla
I used to think that
some antidote against evil spirits
could profoundly change my soul
Carmilla devoted to me her adoration
and I discolored it

I run up to see her
our castle cushioned with
the tapestry of
adventure
we sink into a deep sleep
where I peer into
her rogue and
sullen life
I don't think she will smile

XXVIII
Carmilla

trembling with rage
I will, in a few sentences
close my dreadful story
i am of the old Karnstein family
and if you count me as a vampire
then be my bright moon
ascend shortly after sunset
take my sword
and cut off the burn

place that cordial serenity
against the "hellish arts" which befall us

but you believe in illusions
and I very well know that
you require proof for what you believe
so let me be extraordinary evidence
of that opening before us
laugh, or even smile
with our monsters and
sleep without suspicion
for we are blooming in this pressure

XXIX

Laura

evening arrived in our
secluded quarters
and Carmilla sat looking listlessly on while I
for the first time
had all but obliterated my pride
I was lost and
she smiled in a kind of rapture
so I think I ruined some long ago story

XXX

Carmilla

open my hand
and wish for recovery
in a day or two
this plague shall merely
come down for a picnic
and not long after
set out over the steep Gothic bridge
to ruin castle Karnstein
but our irregularities
lead us to beauty round the broken hollows
inexhaustible is
our old mountain fire

XXXI

Laura

Here is a letter
written under a steep old bridge

our feet reflect the
fading crimson sky
and I love you
Before I lost you
my charm died without
a cause
yet I hope at present there is
a gleam of light to guide me
soon I shall recover
I mean to see you—that is,
if you permit me

so ended this letter
my eyes filled with tears
and it was twilight by the time I returned

a soft clear evening
loitered upon the road
and she had come out

we approached at the drawbridge
and were lost to the shadows
no sweeter scene could be imagined

I heard her profound discourse
eloquent and romantic
she declared a state of brilliancy
in my life
having taken my cheek
she recovered a magnetic influence—and see
i twinkle with that light

XXXII
Carmilla

amuse me with the morning sun
and dance through a crowded saloon
ask me what fear is
when I undertake promises of
departure

I search till two o' clock
for a slight inaccuracy in heaven
I was only too happy, after all, to charm my girl
as she emerged from the trees
How did she lock her perplexities
in mystery

XXXIII

Laura

She said brusquely,
"I think it very sweet how you
hate funerals. Come home."

at the churchyard we buried our ghosts
I hoped only a week ago
as she lay in bed that
our ears shan't be tortured with
discord and jargon
We underwent a change that
alarmed and even terrified me
for we stared down upon suffering
as the hymns dissipated

so we got home
and delicacy passed away
afterwards I witnessed her
as the figure of a wanderer whom I knew very well
with sharp, lean features
smiling from ear to ear
all things I knew mysteriously began to howl
in the midst of the courtyard

XXXIV

Carmilla

on the contrary,
I cannot suspend my
honest assurances from her
I fancied that she spoke of me
hastily kissing her as
the carriage whirled away
We followed the illusion of this place
and were glad to hear
that no one wept
but I publish to the "laity"
the profoundest arcana of our dual existence

here, everything
stands in a forest
and we float on water lilies
Over this Gothic chapel.

Judge whether I say the truth

XXXV

Laura

I am now well assured
that dancing
and resting a little
is our privilege
call me by my name and
let us touch every moment

see me flounder
from one conjecture to another
when criticisms crowd the ballroom
Is that not enough?
do me the kindness
to recognize me?
I should take a chance for
indulgent meditating
you won't deny

XXXVI

Carmilla

We have been very old friends
of God's mercy
I hope the vengeance of Heaven upon
everything that diverges from
the promise

With all my heart
I look forward to
Aladdin's lamp
and fireworks and music
perhaps the world could
throw a rosy light from its early youth on you
so I can wear a mask in the evening
and not question whether she was really watching

XXXVII

Laura

People say I am incapable of infatuation
But my thoughts turn to
coffee and chocolate
i called Carmilla
an anxious disease that
invaded my hospitality
her old-fashioned speech
accompanied her in bed
"Do you think," I said at length,
"that you will ever confide fully in me?"

Carmilla just listened
as dust and ivy rose high above us
she leaned her beautiful face and figure
to me and I
opened up
impatiently repeating
Carmilla, Carmilla, Carmilla
stay here
till we go on

Carmilla is
no doubt
a phenomenon which I
experience as ancient and beautiful
with composure
I think of her unstrung nerves
and reinduce a shadow of curious lore
we remain devoted to
marvelous authentic endings

XXXVIII

Carmilla

Sometimes there came a hand
drawn softly along my cheek
Sometimes warm lips kissed me
longer and more lovingly as I
became conscious
she asked me whether I persisted
in complaining of nerves
for her condition
I said I saw her being murdered
a lamp burned as they learned
the cause of my terror
and if i had her courage
I may fruitlessly
hold our lights aloft and undisturbed

XXXIX

Laura

quite consciously
I consent to her chivalry
it seems predetermined that
she would engage me
and I submit

her beckoning reflects
very ceremoniously
a conviction to title me with
her distinguished name

I remove my mask
and commit myself to kissed hands and
thick velvet cloaks
She touches the carriage with a sigh

look up
I say in the window

She is so beautiful and we
are so renewed

XL

Carmilla

My beloved
several days elapse before
good and pious voices
raise something
profoundly disappointing
so I walk into vitality
ready to seize this note

I place in your hands
another time
another case
But what could be more absurd than
punctures near the throat
and sharp teeth which induce
every symptom of
furnished hallucinations

I remember always
the human symptoms
which made me sustain
the passion of love
in a hundred ways

I will never desist this artful courtship
for you
are a letter in a churchyard
and you smile at journals
written by ghosts
invariably I still bear
the horror of obliteration
but confess to you
in playful
languid
reveries
at the door

XLI

Laura

look down at the river
you said
I rose and walked out into
the night

Are you glad I came?
you asked for the picture you like
How romantic you are, Carmilla
Whenever you are in love
so it should be with you
we glow against all apathy
and take some wine so
Let us look for
the last time at
the strange epidemic that had invaded us
lest we know no weakness

How These Poems Were Created

Everyone who creates erasure poetry has their own process. My method is one of many, but here's how I did it for this collection.

1. I opened the text of *Carmilla* on Project Gutenberg and made my browser window as big as possible. I took screenshots of the text and saved them to my computer. These were my raw pages to work from.

2. I created a blank document where I wrote down words and lines that I wanted to use as I scanned my pages. These became my poems. Often, I built new words by combining individual letters from the original text that appeared in chronological order. For example, if a line in the original text said (bolded for clarity), "**She wa**ited **f**or me at **the s**tream," I could write in my poem "She wafts."

3. I made poems for each page in the book, took a break, then went through all my pages again to make more poems. After two rounds, I had enough material for a collection.

4. I reviewed my poems and decided to combine some or change the order in which they

appeared. Many of the short poems I made from my screenshotted pages became stanzas in longer pieces.

5. I generally did not insert punctuation or change capitalization if it wasn't like that in the original text.

6. Once I had a bunch of pieces that felt like actual poems, I decided which ones seemed more Carmilla and which ones seemed more Laura. I labeled them as such.

7. I did another round where I traced a loose arc of their relationship and figured out the alternating order from there.

Acknowledgements

Thank you for reading. If you enjoyed this collection, please rate and review it. I would also like to thank God, my parents, my church family, and my friends and followers on social media. Your support and encouragement means the world to me.

I'd also like to thank the creative team behind the Carmilla web series, as I would never have learned about Le Fanu's novella without watching and enjoying their take on his story.

About the Author

Taylor Ramage is a poet and sci-fi/fantasy author of Puerto Rican descent. Her short fiction has appeared in speculative and literary anthologies. Her published poetry includes the collections, *Forgive Us Our Trespasses* and *Lest I Know Your Weakness*. Taylor is an avid love of stories in all forms.

Instagram: @taylorrama
Twitter: @TaylorRamage
Tumblr: taylorrama